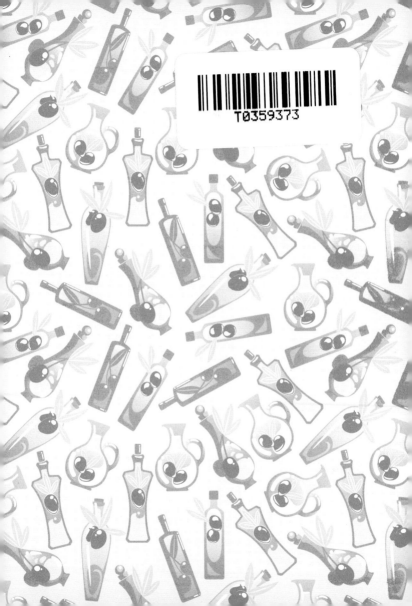

T0359373

Greek

GREEK

Introduction

Greek home cooking and what family meals mean to Greek people are deeply intertwined with tradition, love, and a sense of community. For Greeks, sharing a meal is much more than just eating; it's a way to celebrate life, connect with loved ones, and pass down cultural heritage from one generation to the next.

Greek cuisine is part of the culture of Greece. The most characteristic and ancient element of Greek cuisine is olive oil, which is used in most dishes. It is produced from the olive trees prominent throughout the region which adds to the distinctive taste of Greek food. The olives themselves are also widely eaten. In Greek Cuisine the most important vegetables include tomato, eggplant, potato, green beans, okra, capsicum, and onions.

This book includes some of the most authentic Greek recipes that will take you back to Greece with just one mouth full. From Dolmades which are stuffed Vine Leaves, Baby Octopus, Keftedes which are Meatballs and who doesn't enjoy the sweet taste of Baklava that is just dripping in honey.

Tzatziki
(Cucumber with Yoghurt and Mint)

SERVES 2–4

Ingredients

185 g plain Greek yoghurt
90 g cucumber, grated
1 tablespoon lemon juice
1 clove garlic, crushed
salt and black pepper
1 tablespoon mint chopped, optional

Method

● Combine all the ingredients in a bowl, and season with salt and pepper to taste. Cover with plastic wrap and refrigerate for at least one hour.

● Serve with pita bread as a dip, or as an accompaniment sauce.

Potato Feta Fritters

Ingredients

1½ cups cooked potato, mashed
120 g feta cheese, crumbled
1 egg beaten
3 spring onions, chopped
3 tablespoons fresh dill, chopped
1 tablespoon lemon juice
rind of half a lemon, finely grated
freshly ground black pepper
plain flour, for dredging olive oil
extra dill and lemon, to garnish

Method

● In a medium bowl, add the potato, feta, egg, spring onions, dill, lemon juice, lemon-rind and black pepper. Mix until well combined.

● Cover and chill for 1–2 hours (until firm).

● Using your hands, roll the mixture into golf ball size, flatten slightly. Dredge lightly in flour.

● Heat a little oil in a frying-pan, and cook a few at a time (until golden brown on both sides). Drain on a paper towel and serve at once. Garnish with extra dill and lemon.

Garlic Walnut Sauce

Ingredients

2 slices bread
⅔ cup water
60 g walnuts
2 cloves garlic, roughly chopped
30 ml white wine vinegar
20 ml olive oil
salt and pepper, to taste

Method

- In a small bowl, soak bread in water for 5 minutes, squeeze out water.

- Place walnuts in a food processor and process (until finely chopped). Add bread, garlic and white wine vinegar, and process until combined.

- While motor is running, add olive oil and salt and pepper, process until paste is formed.

- Serve with chicken, fish or vegetables.

Olive Tapenade

SERVES 4

Ingredients

110 g black olives, pitted
⅓ cup parsley
2 cloves garlic, chopped
1 tablespoon capers
¼ cup shallots, sliced
2 tablespoons lemon juice
2 teaspoons oregano
⅓ cup olive oil
salt and ground pepper

Method

● Place olives, parsley, garlic, capers, shallots, lemon juice and oregano in a food processor. Process until well combined.

● With motor running, add olive oil in a slow stream, and process (until a paste has formed). Season with salt and pepper.

Roasted Eggplant and Garlic Dip

MAKES 2 CUPS

Ingredients

1 large eggplant
5 cloves garlic, roasted
olive oil, for drizzing,
plus 1 tablespoon
1 tablespoon tahini
1 tablespoon lemon juice
salt and black pepper

Method

● Pre-heat the oven to 200°C.

● Place the eggplant and garlic on a baking tray, drizzle with olive oil and roast in the oven for 20 minutes. Remove from the oven, scoop the flesh out of the inside of the eggplant, and place the flesh and roasted garlic in the bowl of a food processor.

● Process until puréed, then add the tahini, lemon juice and olive oil, and process for a few seconds to combine.

● Season to taste with salt and pepper, and serve with bread.

Taramosalata
(Fish Roe Purée)

Ingredients

4 slices stale white bread, 3 days old
90g jar taram (red caviar)
185 ml vegetable oil
185 ml olive oil juice of 1 lemon
1 tablespoon water

Method

● Remove crusts from bread and soak the bread in water for 10 minutes. Squeeze bread dry, until all excess water is gone, and place in food processor. Process for 1 minute. Add the taram, and process for another minute.

● With the processor still running, pour the oil in a continuous stream until all the oil has been added and the mixture is creamy and thick.

● Add the juice of the lemon, and the water, and process until well combined. Remove, place in a bowl, and store in the refrigerator for up to seven days.

● Serve with toasted pita bread.

Dolmades
(Stuffed Vine Leaves)

Ingredients

250 g onion, minced

400 g short grain rice

⅔ cup oil

1 tablespoon dill, chopped

½ cup mint, chopped

1 tablespoon salt

150 ml lemon juice

40 small vine leaves

Method

● Mix the onion, rice, oil, herbs, salt and lemon juice in a bowl. Boil some water and soak the vine leaves in boiling water for 15 minutes.

● Then place under cold water for 10 minutes, and lie out on a tea-towel to dry.

● To wrap vine leaves: place one tablespoon of the rice mixture in the centre of the leaf and wrap like a parcel. (Use less mixture if the leaves are small.)

● Place the leaves in a saucepan and cover with boiling water. Add 50 ml of lemon juice to the water. Place a plate over the top of them and cook for an hour (until the vine leaves are cooked).

Baby Octopus marinated in Olive Oil and Oregano

SERVES 4

Ingredients

⅓ cup olive oil
rind of 1 lemon
2 tablespoons lemon juice
⅓ cup shallots, finely sliced
2 teaspoons oregano, chopped
freshly ground pepper and salt
750 g baby octopus, cleaned
salad leaves, for serving

Method

● In a bowl, mix together the olive oil, lemon rind, lemon juice, shallots, oregano, and pepper and salt. Add the octopus and leave to marinate for one hour.

● Heat a chargrill pan, lightly brush with oil, add octopus, and cook (basting with marinade) for 2–3 minutes, or until tender.

● Serve on a bed of salad leaves.

Tiropetes
(Cheese Triangles)

MAKES APPROXIMATELY 25 TRIANGLES

Ingredients

300 g ricotta cheese
300 g feta cheese
4 eggs
white pepper
1 packet filo pastry
125 g melted butter

Method

● Pre-heat oven to 200°C.

● Combine the ricotta, feta and eggs in a bowl and mix well. Season with the white pepper.

● Brush one layer of filo pastry with melted butter, and place another layer on top. Cut the pastry, lengthwise, into 4 strips.

● To shape the triangles,* place a heaped teaspoon of cheese mixture close to the bottom of the right hand corner of the strip.

● Fold this corner over the mixture, diagonally across to the left-hand edge to form a triangle.

● Continue folding from right to left in a triangular shape to the end of strip. Brush top of triangle with melted butter and place on a baking tray. Repeat until all mixture has been used.

● Bake triangles in the oven for about 20 minutes (until they are golden).

* Note: To make larger triangles, cut the strips of pastry wider, and use more filling per triangle.

White Bait Fritters

SERVES 4 (MAKES 20 FRITTERS)

Ingredients

500 g white bait (tiny whitebait)
⅓ cup shallots, finely sliced
2 teaspoons dill, chopped
rind of 2 lemons
2 teaspoons lemon juice
½ cup plain flour
2 eggs, lightly beaten
freshly ground pepper and salt, to taste
olive oil, for frying
lemon wedges

Method

● Place whitebait in a food processor and process until well combined.

● Transfer mixture to a bowl and add shallots, dill, lemon rind, lemon juice, flour, eggs and pepper and salt, and mix together.

● Heat oil in a pan and add mixture (one tablespoon per fritter) and cook for 2–3 minutes (or until golden).

● Serve with wedges of lemon.

Fennel and Zucchini Cakes

SERVES 6

Ingredients

⅔ cup plain flour
1 egg, separated
1 tablespoon olive oil
⅓ cup cold water
¼ teaspoon salt and freshly ground black pepper
250 g fennel bulb
250 g zucchini
1 tablespoon mint, chopped
oil, for shallow frying
garlic flavoured natural yoghurt

Method

● Sift the flour into a bowl and make a well. Into the well add the egg yolk, olive oil and cold water.

● Whisk the centre, gradually incorporating the flour (until a smooth batter has formed). Season with salt and pepper, cover, and leave to thicken for 30 minutes (in a cool place).

cont'd over

Fennel and Zucchini Cakes cont'd

● Grate the fennel and zucchini. Stir (with the mint) into the batter. Whisk the egg-white until soft peaks form, and fold gently into the batter mixture.

● Shallow-fry dessert spoonfuls of mixture (a few at a time). Cook until golden on both sides and cooked in the centre. Drain on paper towels.

● Serve warm with garlic flavoured natural yoghurt.

Eggplant Rolls

Ingredients

2 x 225 g eggplant
3 tablespoons olive oil
3 medium tomatoes,
    seeded and diced
150 g mozzarella
    cheese, finely diced

2 tablespoons fresh
    basil, chopped
salt and freshly ground
    black pepper
fresh basil leaves,
    for serving

Dressing
¼ cup olive oil
1 tomato, diced
1 tablespoon balsamic
    vinegar

2 tablespoons pine
    nuts, toasted

Method

● Remove the stalks from eggplants, and slice
the eggplants lengthwise thinly to thick 5 mm.

● Brush the slices on both sides with oil, and
grill on both sides (until soft and beginning to
brown).

- Pre-heat the oven to 180°C. Combine together (in a bowl) the tomatoes, mozzarella, basil, and seasoning. Spoon a little onto the end of each slice of eggplant, and roll up. Place seam-side down in a greased oven-proof dish, bake for 15–17 minutes.

- In a small pan, using a little of the dressing oil, sauté the tomato until softened. Add the remaining oil, balsamic vinegar and pine nuts, and gently warm. Season to taste. Arrange the rolls on a platter, and spoon the dressing over the rolls.

- Garnish with fresh basil leaves to serve.

Marinated Mushrooms
(Manitaria Marinata)

Ingredients

½ cup olive oil
⅓ cup lemon juice freshly squeezed
½ teaspoon dried thyme
1 stalk fennel, feathery tops
1 clove garlic, crushed
1 stalk celery, finely chopped
10 black peppercorns
1 bay leaf
½ cup water
1 kg fresh small mushrooms
1 lemon
2 tablespoons fresh parsley, chopped for garnish

Method

● In a medium saucepan, combine all of the ingredients down to, but not including, the mushrooms, and bring to the boil. Cover, reduce heat, and simmer until celery is just tender

● Trim off mushroom stems. Cut lemon in halves and run the cut surface of the lemon over the mushrooms. Add mushroom caps to simmering liquid, and cook a further 5 minutes.

● Remove mushrooms with a slotted spoon, and place on serving dish.

● Increase heat, and boil liquid until it reduces and thickens. Pour sauce over mushrooms, cover, cool, and place in refrigerator. Garnish with parsley before serving.

Feta and Ricotta Stuffed Tomatoes

SERVES 6

Ingredients

6 large firm tomatoes
150 g feta cheese, crumbed
150 g ricotta cheese
60 g pine nuts, chopped
10 black olives, stoned and chopped
1½ tablespoons fresh oregano, chopped
3 tablespoons wholemeal breadcrumbs
freshly ground black pepper
6 black olives, to garnish
oregano leaves

Method

● Pre-heat oven to 180°C.

● Cut the top quarters off each tomato, and scoop the centres into a bowl. Dice the tops, and add to the bowl. Combine half the tomato mixture with the feta, ricotta, pine nuts, olives, oregano, breadcrumbs and pepper. Beat mixture together, and spoon back into the cases (piling the tops high).

● Place in a shallow oven-proof dish and bake for 20–25 minutes.

● Garnish with an olive and oregano to serve.

Zucchini and Feta Pie (crustless)

SERVES 6

Ingredients

750 g zucchini

250 g feta cheese

4 eggs, beaten

2 tablespoons toasted walnuts, chopped

2 tablespoons fresh dill, finely chopped

2 tablespoons fresh flat leaf parsley, finely chopped

¼ cup Parmesan, freshly grated

black pepper, freshly ground

1 tablespoon Parmesan, grated, extra

Method

● Trim and wash zucchinis before steaming in a colander for 12–15 minutes (until tender).

● Press out any excess moisture with the back of a wooden spoon.

● Finely chop the zucchinis, and place in a large mixing bowl. Pre-heat oven to 180°C, and grease a 20–24 cm pie dish with butter.

● Soak the feta in warm water for 10 minutes, drain. Mash cheese (until you have a paste like consistency), and add to zucchinis.

- Combine with the remaining ingredients, and stir well.

- Pour into the prepared pie dish, sprinkle with a little extra Parmesan, bake for 45 minutes (or until set). Test the centre with a skewer before serving.

Spanakopeta
(Spinach Pie)

Ingredients

1 bunch English spinach
½ cup olive oil
1½ cups chopped shallots
100 g tasty cheese, grated
1 tbsp fresh dill, chopped
salt and pepper to taste
5 eggs, beaten
16 sheets filo pastry
¾ cup olive oil, for brushing

Method

• Pre-heat oven to 200°C. Cut root end off spinach and wash well. Shred spinach and place in a colander to drain. Shake in a tea towel to dry.

• When dry, place spinach in a large bowl.

● Heat oil in a small pan until very hot. Pour all (but a little) over spinach. This action will wilt the spinach sufficiently. Sauté shallots in remaining oil until soft, and then add to spinach. Mix in both the cheeses, and the dill, salt, pepper and beaten egg.

● Oil a 33 x 25 cm baking dish. Lie a sheet of filo pastry in dish and brush with oil. Repeat until eight sheets have been placed in dish.

● Spread in the spinach mixture, and turn in edges. Cover with eight more sheets, brushing each sheet with oil. Brush top with oil and trim edges. Score top layers of pastry into squares or diamond shapes with a sharp knife. Splash with a little water (to prevent curling).

● Bake in pre-heated oven for ten minutes, then reduce heat to 180°C and bake for 30–35 minutes (until golden brown and puffed). The filling is cooked when the pie puffs up. Do not be deceived into thinking that the pie is cooked if it browns quickly on top. If this is the case, cover the pie with a sheet of brown paper and continue cooking until it comes up like a pillow.

Greek Salad

Ingredients

2 Lebanese cucumbers, sliced

4 Roma tomatoes, quartered

2 Spanish onions, sliced or quartered

80 g feta cheese, crumbled

½ cup Kalamata olives, left whole

3 tablespoons olive oil

2 tablespoon brown vinegar

salt

black pepper, freshly ground oregano leaves, for garnish

Method

● Place all ingredients for the salad in a bowl.

● Combine olive oil and vinegar in a bowl, and whisk. Pour over the salad, then season with salt and ground black pepper.

● Serve salad on its own, or with fresh bread.

● Garnish with oregano leaves.

Lettuce is usually not in a traditional Greek salad, added for extra body and crunch.

Papoutsakia
(Stuffed Eggplants)

Ingredients

4 medium eggplants
salt
oil for frying
2 tablespoons olive oil
1 large onion, finely chopped
2 garlic cloves, crushed
500 g beef or lamb, minced
250 g can tomato pieces, peeled
2 teaspoons tomato paste
2 tablespoons parsley, chopped
⅛ teaspoon nutmeg
½ teaspoon sugar
salt and pepper

Béchamel sauce:

1 tablespoon butter
3 tablespoons plain flour
1½ cups milk
1 egg
salt and pepper
pinch of nutmeg

Method

- Halve eggplants lengthwise. Cut around flesh 5 mm, in from the skin, then make cuts across and down flesh, taking care not to pierce skin.

- Sprinkle cut surface with salt, and stand for 30 minutes. Pat dry and shallow-fry in hot oil for two minutes on each side. Cool a little, then scoop out flesh carefully, leaving a thin wall.

- Reserve flesh, and place cases in an oven-proof dish.

- Heat two tablespoons olive oil in a frying-pan, add onion and garlic, and then sauté until onion is soft.

- Add meat, and while the meat browns, add tomatoes (and their juice), tomato paste, parsley, nutmeg, sugar, salt and pepper.

- Cover and simmer for 20 minutes.

- Add chopped eggplant flesh.

- Fill eggplant cases with mince mixture.

- Prepare béchamel sauce. Pre heat oven to 180°C. Melt butter in a saucepan, add flour, and stir for 1 minute. Gradually add milk, stirring to remove any lumps.

- Cook until it thickens. Remove from heat and quickly add egg while stirring vigorously. Add salt, pepper and nutmeg, and stir over very low heat for 30 seconds.

- Spoon sauce neatly over meat filling. Place in a pre-heated oven and cook for 30 minutes. Remove to serving dish and serve hot as an entrée, or as a main meal.

- Variation: For large eggplants, the béchamel sauce may be omitted, and slices of fresh tomato placed on top of mince. Sprinkle lightly with grated Romano cheese and bake.

Lentil Soup
(Soupa Faki)

Ingredients

500 g lentils
olive oil
2 medium onions, chopped
2 stalks celery, chopped
2 small carrots, chopped
2 cloves garlic, crushed
2 tablespoons tomato paste
2 bay leaves
1 teaspoon oregano, dried
salt
black pepper, freshly ground
½ cup red wine

Method

● Rinse lentils. Heat oil in a large heavy-based stock-pot over medium heat.

● Add onions, celery, carrots, garlic, tomato paste, bay leaves and oregano. Sauté until onions are translucent (4–5 minutes).

● Add lentils and cover with water to a depth of 8 cm. Bring to boil, cover, and reduce heat. Simmer until lentils are tender (about 30 minutes). Check while simmering to ensure lentils are completely covered with water (and add more if necessary).

● Remove from heat, and discard bay leaves. Season with salt, pepper and wine.

● It is best if left standing for a few minutes before serving (to allow flavours to blend).

Lamb Shanks with Broad Beans, Olives and Risoni

SERVES 4–6

Ingredients

2 tablespoons olive oil
2 cloves garlic, crushed
4 lamb shanks
1 onion, chopped
2 cups beef stock
4 sprigs oregano
2 tablespoons tomato paste
2 cups water
1 cup risoni (rice-shaped pasta)
1 cup broad beans*
½ cup olives
2 teaspoons fresh oregano, chopped
salt and freshly ground pepper

Method

● Heat oil in a large saucepan, add garlic, lamb shanks and onion, and cook for five minutes (or until shanks are lightly browned).

● Add the beef stock, sprigs of oregano, tomato paste and half the water, bring to the boil, reduce heat, and leave to simmer (with lid on) for 40 minutes.

● Remove shanks, slice meat off bone, and set aside.

● Add the risoni and water, cook for a further 5 minutes, then add broad beans, olives, meat, oregano and salt and pepper, cook for 5 minutes more, and serve.

* Note: If broad beans are large, peel off outer skin.

Meatballs
(Keftedes)

MAKES 40 MEATBALLS

Ingredients

400 g brown onions,
   finely chopped
1 kg beef mince
½ cup packet
   breadcrumbs
2 eggs
1 tablespoon mint,
   chopped

¼ cup water
salt and freshly ground
   black pepper
plain flour
2 cups vegetable oil,
   for frying

Method

● In a bowl, combine the chopped onion, mince, breadcrumbs, eggs, mint, water and salt and pepper. Using your hands, squeeze the mixture between your fingers making sure it is well combined.

● Using 2 tablespoons of mixture for each meatball, shape into balls, toss in a little flour, shaking off the excess. Flatten each ball slightly into the palm of your hand.

- Heat the oil in a pan* and cook each meatball for approximately 3 minutes (each side) until they are a dark brown colour and cooked through.

- Drain on absorbent paper.

- Serve hot or cold with fresh tomato relish.

* Note: To test the oil for frying, toss a little flour into the oil: when it sizzles, the oil is ready for frying. The meatballs should be flattened out before cooking as they will puff up and rise whilst cooking.

Meatballs in Egg and Lemon Soup
(Youvarlakia)

Ingredients

500g beef mince
1 medium onion, minced
¼ cup parsley, chopped
¼ cup short grain rice
1 egg
salt and pepper
⅓ cup cornflour
1 litre beef stock
50g butter
1 egg
⅓ cup lemon juice

Method

● Combine the mince, onion, parsley, rice and egg in a bowl, and mix well with your hands. Season well with salt and pepper. Using one tablespoon of mixture for each meatball, shape mixture into balls, and roll in cornflour (shaking off the excess).

- Bring the stock and the butter to the boil, then reduce the heat and place the meatballs in the stock. Cover with a lid, and simmer for 45 minutes (until they are cooked). Let cool slightly.

- Whisk the egg and lemon juice together in a bowl, then add 100 ml of warm stock to the egg and lemon juice. Pour this mixture back into the saucepan and heat very gently.

- Season with salt and pepper before serving.

Beef with Artichokes, Olives and Oregano

Ingredients

2 tablespoons olive oil

750g Scotch fillet

1 clove garlic, crushed

1 bunch spring onions, trimmed and halved

½ cup wine

1 cup beef stock

1 tablespoon tomato paste

2 teaspoons oregano, chopped

salt and freshly ground pepper

2 globe artichokes, trimmed, and cut into
    quarters*

⅓ cup olives, pitted

Method

- Pre-heat oven to 180°C.

- In a large heavy-based oven-proof dish heat one tablespoon olive oil, add meat and sear quickly on all sides. Take out and set aside.

- Heat extra olive oil, add garlic and onions, and cook for 2–3 minutes. Add white wine, cook for 1 minute, then add beef stock, tomato paste, oregano, and salt and pepper. Bring to boil, return meat to dish, add artichokes, cover, and bake for 30–40 minutes.

- Add olives in the last 5 minutes of cooking time.

- Slice the meat and arrange with vegetables; pour the sauce over meat and vegetables.

*Note: Trim artichokes of outer leaves and stems. Place in a bowl of water with lemon juice. This stops the artichokes from going brown.

Marinated Lamb Kebabs with Pita, Salad and Yoghurt Sauce
(Arni Souvlakia)

SERVES 4–6
(depending on size of pita bread used)

Ingredients

¼ cup lemon juice
⅓ cup olive oil
1 clove garlic, crushed
1 teaspoon lemon thyme, chopped
salt and pepper
350 g trim lamb, cubed
4 pieces of small pita bread

Salad

1 Lebanese cucumber, cubed
2 Roma tomatoes, quartered
1 Spanish onion, sliced
60 g feta cheese, crumbled
2 tablespoons olive oil
1 tablespoon vinegar
salt and pepper

Yoghurt sauce

200 g natural yoghurt
1 clove garlic, crushed

100 g cucumber, grated
1 teaspoon mint, chopped
salt and pepper to taste

Method

- Combine lemon juice, olive, oil, garlic, lemon thyme and salt and pepper in a bowl, and marinate the lamb for at least 1–2 hours, or overnight (if time permits).

- Combine all salad ingredients in a bowl and set aside.

- Mix all the ingredients for the yoghurt sauce together in a bowl, and set aside.

- Chargrill the lamb pieces for a few minutes each side until lamb is cooked (but still slightly pink). Fill each pita bread with the lamb, salad and yoghurt sauce, and serve warm.

Pastitsio
(Lasagna)

SERVES 10

Ingredients

¼ cup oil
1 onion, sliced
1 kg beef mince
2 tablespoons tomato
   paste
400 g can tomatoes
1 cup water
2 teaspoons oregano,
   chopped
1 teaspoon sugar

1 tablespoon
   Worcestershire sauce
1 cinnamon stick
salt and pepper
400 g penne pasta,
   cooked
2 egg whites
¾ cup grated Romano
   cheese, for the top

Béchamel Sauce

125 g unsalted butter
3 tablespoons plain
   flour

1 litre milk
250 g Romano cheese
4 egg yolks

Method

● Heat the oil and sauté the onion for 5 minutes.
Add the mince meat and cook for 10 minutes,
breaking up the mince (with a fork) as it cooks.

Cont'd over

- Add the tomato paste, tomatoes, water, oregano, sugar, Worcestershire sauce and the cinnamon stick and bring to the boil, then simmer for 45 minutes (until mixture is cooked and sauce is thick). Add more water during cooking if needed.

- Season with salt and pepper.

- To make the béchamel: melt the butter in a saucepan, add the flour, and cook for 3 minutes. Add the milk, and, stirring continuously, bring to the boil, then simmer (until sauce thickens to a good coating consistency). Add the cheese and four egg yolks to the sauce, mixing well, then season with salt and pepper.

- In a large oven-proof dish, layer the cooled penne stirred thru with egg whites then a layer mince meat mixture add as many layers as wanted. Pour the béchamel sauce over the top, sprinkle with the additional cheese, and bake in the oven for 30–45 minutes (until top is golden brown and the Pastitsio is set).

- Serve (cut into slices) hot or cold, with a Greek salad.

Roasted Garlic Lamb
with Rosemary and Risoni

Ingredients

1–1½ kg leg of lamb, trimmed

5 sprigs of rosemary

2 cloves garlic, sliced thinly

¼ cup red wine

2 tablespoons olive oil

1 tablespoon rosemary, chopped

salt

black pepper

risoni

40 ml olive oil

1 clove garlic

1 onion, chopped

1 cup risoni (rice)

1 tablespoon rosemary, chopped

salt and pepper

400 g can tomatoes

1 cup water

Con'd over

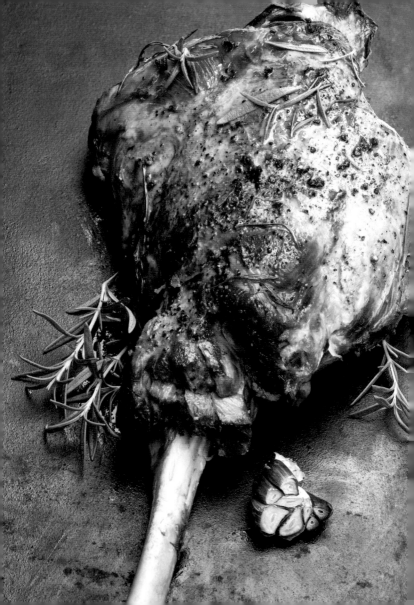

Roasted Garlic Lamb with Rosemary and Risoni (cont'd)

Method

● Pre-heat oven to 220°C.

● Make incisions in the lamb, and place the pieces of sliced garlic, and little sprigs of rosemary, in these incisions.

● Pour the red wine and olive oil over the lamb, sprinkle with chopped rosemary, and season with salt and black pepper.

● To make the risoni, heat oil in a saucepan and sauté the garlic and onion for 10 minutes (until the onion is cooked). Add the risoni and rosemary, season with salt and pepper, then take off heat and set aside.

● Roast the lamb in the oven for 15 minutes, then reduce temperature to 200°C. Roast for a further 45 minutes. Take the lamb out of the oven and add risoni mixture (together with tomatoes and water), and mix well.

● Return lamb to oven for a further 20 minutes until risoni is cooked. (A little more water can be added).

● Serve lamb on a bed of risoni.

Mussels with Tomato Sauce

SERVES 4

Ingredients

1 tablespoon olive oil
1 small onion, finely diced
1 clove garlic, crushed
2 x 400 g canned tomatoes, drained
½ teaspoon sugar
½ teaspoon salt
freshly ground black pepper
3 large basil leaves, roughly torn
1 kg mussels, scrubbed and de-bearded*
extra basil, to garnish

Method

● Heat the oil in a large saucepan and sauté the onion and garlic over a low heat until transparent.

● Add the tomatoes, sugar, salt and pepper. Simmer gently for 20 minutes. Add the basil and keep warm.

● Place the mussels in a large pan with a little boiling water. Cover, and cook over a high heat (until the shells have opened).

● Drain, and then spoon the mussels onto a serving platter accompanied with a bowl of warm sauce in which to dip. Garnish with extra basil leaves.

* Note: When cleaning mussels, discard any which are already opened and any which don't shut when tapped gently. Also discard those that don't open when cooked.

Sword Fish Kebabs with Tomato Sauce

SERVES 4

Ingredients

1 tablespoon olive oil

1 small onion, finely diced

2 cloves garlic, crushed

2 x 400 g canned tomatoes, drained

½ teaspoon sugar

½ teaspoon salt

freshly ground black pepper

750 g swordfish

1 green capsicum, deseeded

1 medium eggplant

6 sprigs rosemary

40 ml olive oil

1 tablespoon rosemary, chopped

salt

Method

- Heat the oil in a large saucepan and sauté the onion and garlic over a low heat (until transparent). Add tomatoes, sugar, salt and pepper.

- Simmer gently for 20 minutes. Add the basil, and keep warm.

- Pre-heat grill or barbecue to moderate.

- Cut swordfish, green capsicum and eggplant into large cubes.

- Arrange on eight skewers (alternating with the rosemary sprigs). Brush with olive oil and chopped rosemary.

- Grill kebabs, turning over at least once to brown the sides. Baste with a little more sauce. The swordfish should be golden, with the herbs and vegetables slightly charred.

- Serve with extra sauce.

Pan-Fried Squid with Lemon
(Kalamaria Tiganita)

SERVES 4

Ingredients

700 g squid tubes
½ cup fine semolina
1 teaspoon salt
1 teaspoon ground pepper
1 cup olive oil, for frying
1 lemon, cut into wedges

Method

• Cut each tube along one side. With a sharp knife score inside skin diagonally in both directions. Cut squid into rectangles, each 2 x 4cm.

• In a bowl, combine the semolina, salt and pepper.

• Heat oil in a large frying-pan or wok. Dip squid into semolina and, when oil is hot, cook a few at a time (until lightly brown and crisp). Drain on absorbent paper and serve with lemon wedges.

Sardines and Chargrilled Capsicum

SERVES 4

Ingredients

1–2 tablespoons olive oil
250 g sardine fillets (16 sardines)
1 tablespoon lemon juice
¼ cup virgin olive oil, extra
40 ml lemon juice, extra
1 tablespoon oregano, chopped
freshly ground pepper and salt
2 red capsicums, roasted and thinly sliced
200 g baby spinach/rocket, washed and trimmed

Method

● Lightly brush chargrill pan with oil, and heat.

● Lightly brush sardines with oil, then add to pan and cook for 1–2 minutes each side.

● Set aside on a plate, and pour 1 tablespoon lemon juice over sardines.

● Combine the olive oil, extra lemon juice, oregano, pepper and salt. Mix until well combined. On a plate (or bowl) add spinach or rocket, add slices of red capsicum, place four sardines on top, and drizzle dressing over sardines.

Seafood Casserole

Ingredients

1 tablespoon olive oil

1 medium onion, roughly chopped

1 leek, finely chopped

2 cloves garlic, crushed

400 g can tomatoes

2 bay leaves

1 tablespoon parsley, chopped

60 ml dry white wine

salt and freshly ground black pepper

1 kg assorted fish and seafood*

2 teaspoons oregano, chopped

Method

● Heat the oil in a flame-proof casserole dish.

● Sauté the onion, leek and garlic until softened and slightly golden.

● Add the tomatoes, bay leaves, parsley, wine, salt and freshly ground black pepper. Bring to the boil, cover, and simmer gently for 20 minutes.

● Stir in any firm-fleshed fish and simmer for 5 minutes.

cont'd over

Seafood Casserole (cont'd)

- Stir in the remaining soft-fleshed fish placing shell fish on the top.

- Cover with a lid and continue cooking for 5–7 minutes (until the fish is tender) and the shellfish have opened (discarding any that remain closed).

- Serve garnished with a fresh bay leaf.

* Note: Suitable fish and seafood include red mullet, monk fish, sea bream, cod, calamari, mussels, shelled prawns and clams.

Baked Sardine Fillets
(Psari Plaki)

Ingredients

1 teaspoon olive oil

185 g sardine fillets

2 tomatoes, peeled and diced

½ green capsicum, deseeded and finely diced

1 teaspoon capers, finely chopped

1 teaspoon fennel, finely chopped

2 teaspoons tomato paste

1 clove garlic, crushed

40 ml lemon juice

salt and freshly ground black pepper

1 tablespoon butter

lemon wedges, to garnish

Cont'd over

Baked Sardine Fillets (cont'd)

Method

● Brush four sheets of aluminium foil with olive oil. Divide sardine fillets into four servings and arrange flat in centre of each foil, skin side down.

● Pre-heat oven to 180°C.

● Combine (in a bowl) the tomato, green capsicum, capers, fennel, tomato paste, garlic, lemon juice, salt and freshly ground black pepper. Mix well, and spoon this over the fillets. Dot with a little butter on the tops, and seal the foil over the fish.

● Bake on a tray for 17 minutes. (Open one to check if the sardines are cooked.)

● Garnish with lemon wedges.

● Serve with a fresh salad.

Baby Salmon in Vine Leaves

SERVES 4

Ingredients

4 fresh baby salmon, cleaned, scaled and gutted
salt and pepper
4 sprigs lemon thyme
4 strips lemon zest
olive oil
8 vine leaves

Sauce
90 ml fruity olive oil
juice of half lemon
1 teaspoon capers, finely chopped
½ teaspoon parsley, finely chopped

Method

● Wash and pat dry the salmon.

● Salt and pepper the cavity before placing a sprig of lemon thyme, and a strip of zest, in each. Rub outside with olive oil, and lightly salt.

● If using fresh vine leaves, trim off the tough part of the vine-stem.

● Blanche in boiling water for 3 minutes, run under cold water, and pat dry. (If using preserved vine leaves, drain, rinse under water, and pat dry).

● Overlap two vine leaves. Place a salmon at one end and roll. Tie with a piece of water-soaked string. Continue with remaining salmon.

● Cook on a pre-heated grill (or barbecue) for 8–12 minutes, turning once during this time.

● Combine the sauce ingredients in a separate bowl, and whisk lightly, just before serving.

Spinach Stuffed Squid

SERVES 4

Ingredients

4 large squid tubes*
2 tablespoons olive oil
1 large onion, chopped
2 x 400 g canned tomatoes, chopped
½ cup white wine
2 bay leaves
2 sprigs of rosemary
extra sprigs of rosemary, for garnish

Stuffing

2 tablespoons olive oil
1 medium onion, peeled and diced
220 g cooked spinach, well drained
½ cup fresh bread crumbs
60 g ricotta cheese
1 clove garlic, crushed
salt and freshly ground black pepper

Method

● To make the stuffing: heat the oil, and pan-fry the onion until softened.

● Remove from the heat, and allow to cool a little before adding the remaining stuffing ingredients. Stir until well blended.

● Rinse and pat dry the squid tubes.

● Divide the stuffing into four, and fill each tube. Secure the ends with metal skewers (or toothpicks).

● Heat the oil in a frying-pan, and soften the onion. Add the tomatoes, wine and herbs. Cook over a medium/high heat (until the mixture becomes pulpy in consistency). Lower the heat to a gentle simmer.

● Add the squid, and spoon some of the mixture over the squid. Season, cover and simmer gently for 30 minutes.

● Take out the skewers, and slice the squid.

● Serve with sauce poured over, and garnished with a little extra rosemary.

*Note: If large squid are unavailable, use 500g of small squid.

Baked Fish
(Psari Plaki)

Ingredients

1½ kg whole snapper or bream
salt and pepper
juice of 1 lemon
½ cup olive oil
1 large onion sliced
3 cloves garlic thinly sliced
½ cup celery chopped
425g can tomato pieces peeled
½ cup dry white wine optional
½ teaspoon sugar
1 teaspoon oregano

Method

● Pre-heat oven to 180°C.

● Prepare fish, leaving head and tail on. Make diagonal cuts on surface, sprinkle with a little salt and pepper and lemon juice. Set aside 20 minutes.

- Heat half the oil in a frying-pan, and sauté onion, garlic and celery for three minutes. Add tomatoes, wine, sugar and oregano, and season with salt and pepper. Sauté a further two minutes.

- Spread mixture into an oiled baking dish and place fish on top. Drizzle remaining oil over fish. Bake in a pre-heated oven 180°C, for 30–40 minutes (depending on size). Baste fish during cooking.

- Remove fish to serving platter, spoon sauce around fish, and serve with vegetable accompaniments or a salad.

Prawns with Spinach

SERVES 4

Ingredients

100 ml olive oil

1 medium onion, diced

1 red capsicum, deseeded and diced

1 clove garlic, crushed

2 tomatoes, peeled and diced

1½ bunches English spinach, washed and
    roughly chopped

2 tablespoons dry white wine

juice of 1 lemon

salt and freshly ground black pepper

500 g prawns, shelled and deveined

lemon wedges to garnish

Method

● Heat two tablespoons of olive oil in a saucepan, and brown onion. Add red capsicum, garlic and tomatoes, and cook for 7 minutes. Add spinach, white wine, lemon juice and seasoning.

● Cover and simmer gently for 8–10 minutes (until spinach is tender).

● Take off heat. Stir and keep warm.

- Add the remaining oil to a large frying-pan.

- Once hot, add prawns and sauté, stirring constantly, for 3 minutes (or until just cooked).

- Spoon the prawns into the spinach, fold to combine, and spoon onto a warm serving platter, garnished with lemon wedges. Serve immediately.

Green Beans in Tomato Sauce
(Fasolia Ya Hni)

Ingredients

500g green beans, fresh
65mL olive oil
1 medium onion, chopped
1 clove garlic, crushed
1 cup oz water
425g can tomato pieces, peeled
1 tablespoon tomato paste
1 teaspoon sugar
½ teaspoon salt
1 teaspoon oregano, dried

Method

- Wash beans, top and tail.

- Heat oil in a saucepan, and sauté onion and garlic until onion is soft, but not brown.

- Add water, bring to boil, add beans, boil for 5 minutes.

- Add tomatoes, tomato paste, sugar, salt and oregano. Turn down heat and simmer for 25–30 minutes (until beans are tender and sauce has reduced).

Rice with Lemon, Dill and Spinach

SERVES 4

Ingredients

2 tablespoons olive oil
1 brown onion, chopped
garlic, 1 large bunch
silver beet, washed and shredded
1 cup of short grain rice
1½ cup chicken stock
1 bunch dill, chopped
juice and rind of 1 lemon

Method

● Heat oil, add the onion and garlic, and cook for one minute. Add silver beet, cook until silver beet just wilts.

● Add the rice and stir through. Add the stock, reduce the heat, and cover for 10 minutes.
If liquid has evaporated (and rice needs more cooking), add a little more water and cook for a further few minutes.

● When rice is cooked, add chopped dill and lemon juice, season before serving.

Roasted Herb-Stuffed Chicken
(Kota Yemista)

SERVES 4–6

Ingredients

4 chicken breasts, skin on
2 tablespoons thick natural yoghurt
1 clove garlic, crushed
1 teaspoon olive oil
2 tablespoons mint, finely chopped
2 tablespoons flat leaf parsley, finely chopped
2 tablespoons oregano, finely chopped
2 tablespoons thyme, finely chopped
2 tablespoons fennel, finely chopped
2 spring onions, finely chopped
salt and finely ground black pepper

Method

- In a small bowl combine together all the ingredients* (except the chicken) and mix well.

- Using your finger tips, scoop up a quarter of the mixture and gently push under the skin of the chicken. Run your fingers over the skin to smooth the stuffing out. Repeat with the remaining pieces.

- Cover, and refrigerate for 1½ hours.

- Pre-heat the oven to 180°C, place the chicken on a roasting rack, and cook chicken for 15–17 minutes. (When juices run clear, the chicken is cooked.)

* Note: The herbs all need to be very finely chopped.

Chicken Kebabs with Yoghurt and Lemon Sauce

SERVES 4

Ingredients

300 g plain yoghurt

2 clove garlic, crushed

1½ teaspoon paprika, ground

1½ teaspoon cumin seeds

1 small red capsicum, cut into squares

¼ cup lemon juice

2 tablespoons parsley, chopped

2 teaspoons oregano, chopped

freshly ground pepper

6 chicken thigh fillets, cubed

24 satay sticks

Method

- Soak satay sticks in cold water for 30 minutes.
- Place (in a bowl) yoghurt, garlic, paprika, cumin seeds, lemon juice, parsley, oregano and pepper, and mix until combined.
- Place chicken and capsicum on satay sticks and brush-over with half the mixture. Leave to marinate in refrigerator for 2–3 hours.
- Heat oil on barbecue (or chargrill pan), add chicken kebabs and cook 4–5 minutes each side.
- Serve with remaining marinade mixture.

Chicken, Roasted Capsicum, Olive and Feta Pie

SERVES 4–6

Ingredients

2 tablespoons olive oil
1 large leek, washed and sliced
1 clove garlic, crushed
500 g chicken breasts, diced
1 bunch English spinach, washed and blanched
2 red capsicum, roasted and diced
50 g black olives, pitted and halved
200 g feta cheese, crumbled
2 tablespoons parsley, chopped
1 tablespoon oregano, chopped
3 eggs
¼ cup cream
freshly ground pepper
8–16 sheets filo pastry
1 tablespoon olive oil, extra
1 tablespoon butter, melted
1 tablespoon sesame seeds

Method

● Pre-heat oven to 180°C.

● Heat one tablespoon oil in a large frying-pan, add leek and garlic, and cook for 5 minutes (or until soft). Set aside.

- Heat extra oil, add chicken in batches, and cook for 6–8 minutes.

- Drain spinach, squeeze out excess water, and chop roughly.

- In a large bowl, combine chicken, spinach, capsicum, olives, feta, parsley, oregano, eggs, cream and pepper. Stir until well combined. Set aside.

- Lightly grease a 22 x 22 cm square baking dish.

- Combine the extra oil and butter. Lay out sheets of filo, put two together, and brush with the oil mixture. Put another two on top, and brush again. Continue to repeat this (until you have four double sheets).

- Line the baking dish with the filo, and trim around the edges. Fill with the chicken mixture. Brush the remaining sheets with oil (the same as before, using the same amount). Place the filo on top of the baking dish, tucking the edges inside.

- Brush the top with the oil mixture, sprinkle with sesame seeds, and bake in the oven for 40–45 minutes.

Greek Style Chicken Rissoles in Tomato Sauce

SERVES 4–6

Ingredients

Rissoles

500 g chicken mince
1 medium onion, grated
2 tablespoons parsley, finely chopped
½ teaspoon salt
pepper
1 egg
½ cup breadcrumbs, dried
1 tablespoon water
oil, for frying

Tomato sauce

1 medium onion, finely chopped
1 clove garlic, crushed
1 tablespoon oil
440 g can tomatoes
1 tablespoon tomato paste
½ cup water
½ teaspoon oregano, dried
1 teaspoon sugar
salt and pepper
1 tablespoon parsley, chopped

Method

● Place chicken mince in a bowl, grate onion into the mince, and add remaining ingredients. Mix well to combine, and knead a little by hand. With wet hands roll into balls. Heat oil 1 cm deep, in a frying-pan, and sauté the rissoles (until they change colour on both sides). Remove to a plate.

● For the sauce, add to the pan the onion and garlic, and sauté a little. Add remaining sauce ingredients, and bring to the boil.

● Return rissoles to the pan, reduce heat, and simmer (covered) for 30 minutes.

● Serve over boiled spaghetti (or preferred pasta).

Spinach, Olive and Feta Frittata with Roasted Capsicum Sauce

SERVES 4–6

Ingredients

10 eggs
1 tablespoon fresh oregano, chopped
black pepper, freshly crushed
¼ cup olive oil
200g potatoes, peeled and diced
1 brown onion, diced
1 clove garlic, crushed
150g baby spinach
60g pitted Kalamata olives, halved
80g feta, crumbled
60g semi-dried tomatoes
3 large red capsicums

Method

● Lightly whisk together the eggs and oregano in a bowl, and season with black pepper. Set aside.

● Heat the oil in a 22cm pan and sauté the potato, onion and garlic for a few minutes (until soft).

• Add the spinach and cook (until spinach begins to wilt). Remove the pan from the heat, then add olives, feta and semi-dried tomatoes.

• Return the pan to a very low heat, pour in the egg mixture, and cook for 10–15 minutes. Run a spatula around the sides of the pan as the frittata is cooking, and tilt it slightly whilst cooking (so that egg mixture runs down the sides a little).

• When frittata is almost cooked through the middle, place under a grill for five minutes to cook and brown the top.

• Serve in wedges with the roasted capsicum sauce.

For the Sauce:
• Halve the capsicums and remove the seeds. Chargrill the capsicums (or grill) until black. Let them cool, and remove the skins. Place into a food processor and process until puréed. Transfer to a bowl. Makes 1 cup.

Lemon and Yoghurt Semolina Cake

SERVES 6–8

Ingredients

125 g butter, softened
¾ cup caster sugar
rind from 1 lemon,
    finely grated
4 eggs
1 cup fine semolina

2 teaspoons baking
    powder
1 cup almond meal
1 cup raisins
½ cup almonds, flaked
200 g yoghurt

Syrup

1 cup caster sugar
1 cup lemon juice

½ cup honey

Method

● Pre-heat oven to 180°C.

● Grease a 20 cm cake tin, and line with paper.

● In a large bowl, add butter, sugar and rind.

● Using an electric beater, cream butter, sugar and rind until light and soft.

● Add eggs one at a time, and beat well after each egg.

Cont'd over

Lemon and Yoghurt Semolina Cake Cont'd

● Fold in semolina, baking powder and almond meal. Lightly fold in raisins, almonds and yoghurt.

● Pour mixture into prepared cake tin and bake for 35–45 minutes (or until cake is lightly browned on top).

● To make the syrup, in a small saucepan combine sugar, lemon juice and honey. Cook on a low heat for 15–20 minutes (or until it forms a syrup).

● Using a skewer, poke cake evenly. Cool syrup slightly, and pour over cake. Serve with cream.

Almond Shortbread Biscuits

MAKES 20 BISCUITS

Ingredients

400 g butter, clarified
50 g caster sugar
1 tablespoon vanilla essence
100 g roasted blanched almonds
1 egg yolk
5 cups plain flour
cloves
icing sugar

Method

● Pre-heat the oven to 170°C.

● Beat the butter with the sugar until pale and creamy, then add the vanilla and yolk and mix until well combined. Sift flour and fold into the mixture with a metal spoon (until well combined). Bring the dough together with your hands, and knead lightly for two minutes (until smooth). Wrap in plastic, and refrigerate for 15 minutes.

cont'd over

Almond Shortbread Biscuits cont'd

● Flatten-out the dough with your hands (to a thickness of 1–2 cm), and roll–into half moon shapes. Place a clove in the centre of each biscuit, and bake on a baking sheet for 15 minutes (or until biscuits are golden).

● Remove from the oven, place on a sheet of bakewell paper and (while still hot) sift icing sugar over biscuits (until well covered). Let them cool, and store in an airtight container.

Baklava

Ingredients

250 g unsalted butter, melted

400 g blanched roasted almonds, ground

1½ teaspoons cinnamon

½ cup caster sugar

700 g filo pastry

Syrup

3 cups caster sugar

1½ cups water

1 cinnamon stick

1 piece of orange or lemon rind

1 tablespoon honey

Method

- Pre-heat oven to 275°C.

- Melt butter, set aside.

- Mix nuts in a bowl, with cinnamon and sugar.

- Brush baking tray 25 x 33 cm with the butter.

- Place one sheet of filo on bottom of dish with ends hanging over sides. Brush with melted butter and add another layer of filo. Repeat with 8 more filo sheets.

- Sprinkle nut mixture generously over the filo.

- Continue the layering of filo pastry (3 sheets) and one layer of nuts until all nuts are used.

● Top with 8 reserved sheets of filo, making sure the top sheet is well buttered. Cut the top lengthwise in parallel strips.

● Bake in oven at 275°C for 30 minutes, then reduce heat to 150°C and bake for a further hour.

● To make the syrup, place ingredients in saucepan and bring to the boil. Reduce heat and let simmer for 10–15 minutes. Leave to cool before use. Pour cold syrup over baklava and cut into diamond shapes.

Almond Cakes

Ingredients

500 g almonds, blanched
1 cup caster sugar
2 medium eggs
20 g soft white bread crumbs
⅓ cup liquid honey

Method

● Grind almonds in a food processor (with a little of the sugar). Combine the remaining sugar with the eggs, and whisk until pale and creamy. Add the ground almonds to the bread crumbs, and stir until well combined.

● Pre-heat oven to 180°C.

● Shape (using a tablespoon) roughly into diamond shapes, and place on a non-stick baking tray. Bake for 15 minutes.

● Whilst warm, place on wire cooling racks, and brush with warm honey. Leave to cool a little before serving.

Greek Shortbread
(Kourabiethes)

Ingredients

250 g butter, unsalted

2 tablespoons icing sugar

1 tablespoon brandy

½ cup almonds, chopped

2⅓ cups plain flour, sifted

1 teaspoon baking powder

whole cloves

rose water

500 g icing sugar, sifted

Method

● Cream butter (until white and fluffy). Add icing sugar, and brandy.

● Stir in almonds and half the sifted flour. Use your hand to mix in remaining flour (a little at a time), and mix to a soft dough. If dough is sticky, add a little more flour.

● Break off pieces and roll into a ball, flatten slightly in the palm of your hand, then pinch twice leaving four fingerprints. Insert a clove in top of each if desired, place on ungreased baking sheet.

- Bake in a pre-heated moderate oven 180°C for 15–20 minutes (until lightly coloured, but do not brown). Remove from oven, and stand for 5 minutes. Splash a little rose water over the biscuits.

- Sift icing sugar onto a large sheet of grease-proof paper or a large tray. Lift warm biscuits onto this, then completely cover with icing sugar. Allow to cool in icing sugar.

Butter Cookies
(Koulouria)

Ingredients

125 g butter
125 g ghee
1¼ cups caster sugar
½ teaspoon cinnamon, ground
3 eggs
⅓ cups brandy
1½ teaspoons baking powder
4–5 cups plain flour
sesame seeds
egg glaze

Method

● Cream butter, ghee and sugar well, and add cinnamon. Gradually add eggs, beating mixture well.

● Add brandy and baking powder, then begin to add flour. Add as much as is needed to make a stiff (not dry) dough. It is safer to add half the flour, then mix in a little at a time (until desired consistency is reached). Test to see if dough is right by rolling a little in your hands: if it is not sticky, and rolls well, enough flour has been added.

● Shape pieces of dough into slim pencil-shapes, roll into sesame seeds, form into twists, circles or scrolls. Place on greased baking sheet, glaze with egg glaze, bake in moderately hot oven 190°C for 15–20 minutes. Cool on wire rack.

Index

First published in 2024 by New Holland Publishers
Sydney

Level 1, 178 Fox Valley Road, Wahroonga, NSW 2076, Australia

newhollandpublishers.com

A record of this book is held at the National Library of Australia.

ISBN 9781760797751

Managing Director: Fiona Schultz
Olga Dementiev: General Manager/Publisher
Author: David Cowie
Designer: Andrew Davies
Production Director: Arlene Gippert
Printed in China

Keep up with New Holland Publishers:

NewHollandPublishers
@newhollandpublishers

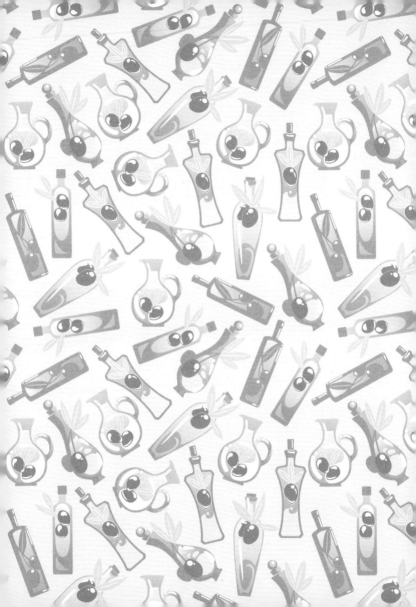